Cooking in a CAN

More Campfire Recipes for Kids

KATHERINE L. WHITE

Illustrated by
Debra Spina Dixon

Gibbs Smith, Publisher
Salt Lake City

Palos Heights Public Library
12501 S. 71st Avenue
Palos Heights, IL 60463

J
641.5
WHI
DD

For my mom, whose path I follow, and my dad,
who teaches me to tread gently — KW

For my husband, John — DD

First Edition
10 09 08 07 06   5 4 3 2 1

Text © 2006 Katherine L. White
Illustrations © 2006 Debra Spina Dixon

All rights reserved. No part of this book
may be reproduced by any means
whatsoever without written permission
from the publisher, except brief por-
tions quoted for purpose of review.

Published by
Gibbs Smith, Publisher
P.O. Box 667
Layton, Utah 84041

Orders: 1.800.748.5439
www.gibbs-smith.com

Designed by Dawn DeVries Sokol
Printed and bound in Hong Kong

Disclaimer: The publisher and author assume no responsibility for any damages or injuries incurred
while performing any of the activities in this book; neither are they responsible for the results of
these recipes or projects.

Library of Congress Cataloging-in-Publication Data

White, Katherine L.
    Cooking in a can : more campfire recipes for kids ; illustrated by Debra Spina Dixon /
Katherine L. White.—1st ed.
    p. cm.
ISBN 1-58685-814-9
1. Outdoor cookery. 2. Cookery, American. I. Title.
TX823.W47 2006
641.5'78—dc22   2005033526

contents

introduction

Did you ever boil water for hot chocolate in a paper cup? Cook breakfast in a paper bag? Bake a cake underground? In this book, you'll learn to cook in leaves, in orange peels, and on rocks. You'll make a tin-can grill, an underground oven, and a solar cooker.

The recipes in this book have simple ingredients, clear cooking instructions, and thorough safety guidelines to make every camp-cooked meal a success. The book also includes basic campfire instructions and fun activities. Each recipe can be adapted for cooking in your backyard, at the seashore, or in the woods. What are you waiting for? It's time for some campfire cooking fun!

planning & packing

Planning ahead will help make your campfire cooking go more smoothly, whether you are cooking in the backyard on the grill or traveling to a favorite family campground. This chapter will help you get organized and pack for your cookout.

WHERE THERE'S SMOKE THERE'S FIRE!

The risk of forest fires is always present, and it is higher in the summertime. Some parks, counties, and states limit the

kinds of fires you can have, and when and where you can have them. Most fire bans are for wood fires. If your area has a high fire danger, you might need to use gas or charcoal grills rather than having an open

fire pit. Have an adult help you find out what kinds of fires are okay in your area.

SAFETY FIRST *Safety is your most important responsibility. An adult should be with you at all times when you are cooking or doing activities in this book. Many of the activities involve intense heat or sharp knives. In those cases, use extra caution.*

MAKE A PLAN

Before you head to the backwoods, beach, or park, you need to prepare. There's nothing like having a nice fire and a sharpened stick only to realize you have no marshmallow! Make a menu of what meals you want to serve each day. Then make a shopping list.

PACKING LIST

Here's a sample packing list of things you might want to take.

For cooking:

- Aluminum foil
- Shovel
- Can opener
- Knife
- Long-handled tongs and turner
- Oven mitts
- Measuring cups and spoons

- Resealable plastic bags
- Wire grill
- Pots, pans, or coffee cans
- Pitcher or bucket
- Bucket of dirt or sand
- Heat-proof spatula or wooden spoon
- Matches
- Portable kitchen timer or wristwatch

For cleanup:

- Plastic grocery and trash bags
- Washtub

- Dishcloth
- Biodegradable soap

For eating:

- Dishes (paper or reusable)
- Silverware (plastic or regular)
- Napkins
- Cups (paper, plastic, Styrofoam, or tin)
- Table cover
- Drinks

- Salt, pepper, ketchup, salsa, and other condiments

Miscellaneous:

- Ice chest or insulated container with ice packs
- First aid kit
- Flashlight
- Camera
- Insect repellent
- Sunscreen

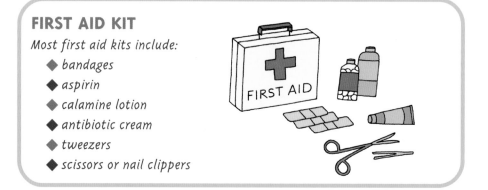

FIRST AID KIT

Most first aid kits include:

- *bandages*
- *aspirin*
- *calamine lotion*
- *antibiotic cream*
- *tweezers*
- *scissors or nail clippers*

Make a Cooking Apron

What you need:

◆ a pair of old jeans (they don't need to fit)
◆ scissors
◆ measuring tape
◆ needle and thread
◆ two old neckties or a belt

What you do:

1. Cut the legs off the jeans, about 2 inches below where the insides of the pockets end.

2. Ask an adult to turn the jeans inside out and help you sew across each cutoff leg. Sew through the zipper placket, stitching it closed. Turn the pants back outside out. They should look more like a bag now, with two large pouches plus pockets for keeping your cooking utensils handy.

3. Put a belt around your waist, insert it through the back belt loops of your apron, and then fasten the buckle. Or, tie one necktie to each side belt loop, pull the apron to you, and then tie the neckties behind your back.

Create a Campfire Cooking Notebook

Take a notebook with you to record your camp cooking adventure. Use a lined notebook you get from the grocery store, a hand-bound nature journal from a bookstore or the ranger station, or anything in between. You can even make your own notebook by stapling or sewing pages of paper together. Decorate your notebook with drawings or stickers. Make rubbings of trees or leaves. Draw a picture of the lake. Go wild!

Write the date of your cookout, what you cooked, and how it turned out. Ask friends and family to write about the trip too.

Setting up camp

Today, companies make and sell waffle irons, coffeemakers, and even ovens to use outdoors. While you may eventually want a few of these gadgets, they're not necessary. For thousands of years families have been cooking and eating outside without a lot of fancy equipment. You can too! With practice and a little help, you can whip up an outdoor feast that will impress even experienced cooks.

KEEPING FOOD COOL

Milk, cheese, meat, and some other foods must stay cold until you cook or eat them, or else they can make you sick. Other things, like fruit and drinks, just taste better cold. Chocolate bars may not normally need to be refrigerated, but they'll be chocolate soup if packed in a hot car and not kept cool.

You can carry food that needs to be kept cool to your cook site in a plastic ice chest or insulated container with some ice packs or resealable plastic bags filled with ice. If you plan on having leftovers, bring enough ice to keep extra food cold until it's eaten.

Cool fruit can make a tasty treat on a hot summer day. A chilled orange, bunch of grapes, or slice of watermelon are refreshing after-hike snacks.

NATURAL REFRIGERATION

Once you get to your campsite, you may be able to use natural refrigeration to keep some foods cool. If there is a lake or stream nearby (that's not too deep or too swift), bundle up your fruit in a plastic sack, bucket, or crate and set it into a slow, shallow spot in the water. Anchor your container with rocks or lash it to a tree so it doesn't wash away. Use this method for foods that can be peeled and the peel thrown away—never eat the part that touches the water. So, for example, bananas or string cheese sealed in plastic are okay, but apples or lunchmeat aren't, unless they're tightly sealed in plastic bags or containers.

LEARN TO IMPROVISE

Even when you plan and pack carefully, every once in a while you will probably forget something. If you're left without some supplies, improvise! A few layers of aluminum foil can be folded into a bowl, plastic bags can make plates, and clean hands can do a lot of things silverware can.

Many campsites and parks have general stores with the bare essentials. Pay a visit to replace the things that simply have no substitute like marshmallows and chocolate bars.

SAFE DRINKING WATER

Rivers, lakes, and oceans are wonderful places to dip your feet, cool a watermelon, or sit by. But no matter how refreshing the water looks, never drink it! Ocean water is too salty to drink, and most lakes and rivers carry bacteria called *giardia,* (gee-ARE-dee-a) which can make you very sick. Many parks have pumps or spigots with drinkable water, but unless you know this ahead of time, it's best to bring your own water or a way to treat unsafe water.

◆ Bottled water is widely available. But with all the cooking, washing, and drinking you'll be doing, it can get expensive.

◆ Most grocery, retail, or outdoor stores sell reusable water bottles or canteens to fill at home and take with you.

◆ There are many options for water treatment, including chemicals and filters.

◆ The cheapest way to purify water is to boil it for ten minutes.

CAMP CLEANUP

After devouring your meal, it's time to clean up—wash dishes, throw away garbage,

store food, and set aside recycling. Any time you leave your campsite or go to bed, your space should be spotless. Litter ruins nature for others and invites unwanted visitors like bears. The good news is that cleanup is much more fun in the wilderness than at home!

Create a Family Banner

It's fun to stake out your camp area with a family banner. Craft stores sell poster board, rolls of paper, fabrics, and sometimes premade pennants and banners ready for painting.

CAMPBELL COOKOUT
2008

THE
DIXON
FAMILY

You'll also find the markers, paint, stickers, and stencils to help you identify your camp or picnic area. Paint your family's name or crest, and announce your name or theme. When your banner is done, tie it between two trees or hang it on the edge of the picnic table.

campfires

Whether you're cooking in aluminum foil, a paper bag, or a pot, the one thing you absolutely need is heat. Your kitchen at home probably has a few different ways of heating things—the stovetop, oven, microwave, toaster, and so on. You can use a variety of heating methods at camp, too. Most camp cooks, in both the backyard and backwoods, like to cook over an old-fashioned campfire, but they also enjoy the convenience of a charcoal fire, gas-powered camp stove, or backyard grill.

RULES FOR FIRE SAFETY

Being smart about fire safety helps keep everyone safe.

◆ Always have an adult helper with you when you're using fire.

◆ Never leave a fire unattended.

◆ Build fires in a pit, an existing fire ring, or a fire ring you make with larger rocks, cinder blocks, or bricks placed in a circle on flat ground. Put stoves, grills, and other heat sources on flat, heat-resistant surfaces that are clear of grass, pinecones, paper, or anything else that could catch fire.

◆ A smaller fire is easier to control and is better for cooking.

◆ Never use outside equipment inside. Camp stoves and the stoves used in this book are all meant to be used outdoors.

◆ Always keep a shovel and a bucket of water or sand nearby. You'll need these to put out the fire when you're finished cooking or if it gets too big.

◆ Make sure the fire is *completely* out when you're finished. Ask an adult to check.

GATHERING FUEL

Fuel burns to create heat. The fuel used in a traditional campfire is wood. To build a campfire, you'll need three types of fuel:

- ◆ **tinder** (like pinecones, small twigs, or dry bark)
- ◆ **kindling** (bigger sticks)
- ◆ **main fuel** (logs)

Make a fire by putting tinder on the bottom. Then add kindling on top of that. Then add logs.

In some places, wood gathering is not allowed. You may need to bring your own wood or buy it at a camp or convenience store. If you do collect firewood, take only what is already on the ground. Just make sure that the log isn't a wild critter's home!

BUILDING THE FIRE

Once you know it's okay to have a campfire, and you've cleared the area and collected your wood, you're ready to build a fire. There are many different kinds of fires to cook over. One great one is the log cabin fire. This kind of fire burns slowly and leaves a thick bed of hot coals, which means you have a fire that stays the perfect temperature for cooking for a long time.

To build a log cabin fire:

1. Pile a handful of tinder in the middle of your fire pit.

2. Lean kindling over the tinder, making a teepee shape.

3. Stack logs in a square around the teepee. As your stack gets taller, gradually place the logs closer to the kindling.

4. Keep stacking until the "log cabin" comes up to your knees.

5. Using a match, carefully light the tinder. It takes 20 to 30 minutes for the fuel to burn to coals. Keep an eye on the fire—when the flames disappear and the wood turns red with white ash edges, you're ready to cook.

COOKING TIME

Remember, altitude (how high up you are from sea level) affects cooking time. If two people cook the same food over identical fires—one on an ocean beach and the other high in the mountains—the chef on the beach will finish cooking first.

Also, fires made of different woods burn differently. Some burn hotter or faster than others. The cooking times given in this book are averages. Your food may cook a little faster or a little slower than the time listed.

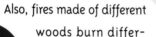

PUTTING OUT THE FIRE

When you're ready to leave your campsite or turn in for the night, use your shovel and bucket and put out the fire.

◆ With the shovel or a stick, spread the coals into a thin, even layer.

◆ Dribble water, dirt, or sand onto the coals. Pour slowly! Dumping water on all at once will fling sparks into the air and out of the fire ring. It could even burn you with steam. Besides, a slow dribble on the fire makes a cool sizzle.

◆ When the coals appear to be out, carefully stir them, and then repeat the process. Make sure your adult helper agrees the fire is completely out.

Make a Sweatshirt Wood Carrier

A wood carrier makes gathering kindling and tinder for your fire a whole lot easier. If you are allowed to collect wood at your site, try this out.

What you need:

◆ an old sweatshirt or long-sleeved shirt

What you do:

1. Spread your shirt on the ground, with the arms stretched out.

2. Place sticks of wood up and down (not across) the torso of the shirt.

3. When you have about two armfuls of wood laid on the shirt, pull the sleeves in tightly and tie a knot. The shirt should hug the wood.

4. Hoist your bundle onto your back, using the sleeves to hold on to. Or you can tie the shirt around your waist or shoulders.

Now your hands are free to pick up extra wood or litter on the way back to camp!

A BUNDLE OF FIRE STARTERS

Sometimes dry kindling is hard to find. You can make these fire starters at home to take with you on your camp cookout. Store them in a waterproof container or self-zipping plastic bag until you need them. To use the fire starters, place one on a crumpled sheet of newspaper and lay firewood on top. Once you light the newspaper, you'll soon be cooking!

Newspaper Fire Starters

What you need:

◆ newspaper
◆ 6 pieces of string, about 12 inches long each
◆ scissors
◆ melted wax (see page 23)
◆ wax paper

What you do:

1. Melt wax according to directions on page 23.

2. Roll up a sheet of newspaper the long way.

3. Every 3 or 4 inches, tie a string around it.

4. Cut the newspaper between the strings, so you have small tied bundles of newspaper.

5. Hold the end of the string and lower the newspaper into the pot of hot wax. When you pull it out of the wax, hold it over the pot for a few seconds until it stops dripping. Then lay it on the wax paper to dry.

6. Trim the string to a few inches.

Pinecone Fire Starters

What you need:

- ◆ pinecones
- ◆ 1 piece of string, about 10 inches long, for each pinecone
- ◆ newspaper
- ◆ potholder or trivet
- ◆ melted wax (see page 23)

What you do:

1. Tie a piece of string around each pinecone. Leave about a 6-inch tail.

2. Spread some newspaper on a flat surface and place the potholder or trivet on it.

3. Melt wax according to directions on page 23. Using an oven mitt, place the container of melted wax on the potholder.

4. Holding the tail of the string, dip the pinecones one at a time into the wax.

5. After the pinecones are coated, place them on the newspaper until they are dry.

EGG CARTON FIRE STARTER

What you need:

◆ sawdust or newspaper

◆ cardboard egg carton*

◆ melted wax (see page 23)

Note: Never burn Styrofoam or plastic!

What you do (if using newspaper):

1. Shred the newspaper and fill each egg cup with the shredded pieces.

2. Melt wax according to directions on page 23.

3. Pour wax into newspaper-filled egg carton.

4. Let the fire starter harden and cool.

What you do (if using sawdust):

1. Melt wax according to directions on page 23.

2. Stir the sawdust into the melted wax.

3. Carefully pour the hot wax-and-sawdust mixture into each cup of the egg carton.

4. Let the fire starter harden and cool.

Melting Wax

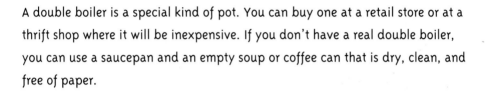

You can buy wax at a craft store. It comes in blocks. Use
$1/2$ pound of wax (also called paraffin) for each set of fire
starters. Be careful! Wax catches fire if it gets too hot. Its
ability to burn will allow you to start a fire with it later. Have
an adult helper with you.

A double boiler is a special kind of pot. You can buy one at a retail store or at a
thrift shop where it will be inexpensive. If you don't have a real double boiler,
you can use a saucepan and an empty soup or coffee can that is dry, clean, and
free of paper.

What you do:

1. Fill a 2- or 3-quart saucepan about halfway with water.

2. Put it on the stove on high heat until the water comes
   to a boil. Then turn the heat down to medium-low.

3. Put your solid wax in the top part of the double boiler or in the
   can. Carefully place this part into the water, making sure
   water doesn't get in with your wax.

4. Stir the wax gently with a spoon as it melts.
   When the wax is completely liquid, turn off
   the stove.

5. Using an oven mitt, remove the can or pot from the water and place it
   on a potholder. Use the melted wax to make your fire starters.

cooking on outdoor stoves

It's fun to cook right over an open fire, but there may be times when you can't have a fire. Maybe there is a forest fire watch prohibiting open campfires or maybe you want to do a cookout in your own backyard or at a nearby park where fires aren't allowed. Gas grills, camp stoves, and charcoal grills are other great options for outdoor cooking.

GAS GRILLS AND CAMP STOVES

Gas-powered stoves and grills adjust easily for cooking from low (for keeping soup warm) to high (for boiling water), and anything in between. Grills come in many different shapes and sizes, and use different fuel types like propane or kerosene. All have wire racks for cooking meat, vegetables, or a dessert.

Camp stoves are portable, gas-powered stoves that have one to three burners. They work best when you are cooking something in a pot or pan like on your stovetop at home.

CHARCOAL GRILLS

Charcoal is another kind of fuel. You can make a charcoal fire in your backyard or at a campsite and cook your food over it on an existing grill or one you make yourself. Charcoal lights faster than wood, so you only need tinder (usually lighter fluid or paper) and the main fuel (charcoal briquettes). Remember to build the fire in the body of the grill and don't forget your fire safety rules!

Remove the wire rack and build the fire in the body of the grill. On the underside of many grills, there is a vent that opens and closes with a handle—open this vent before starting the fire. When you're finished with the fire, close the vent to cut off the supply of oxygen.

EGG CARTON BRIQUETTE FIRE STARTER

Use a paper egg carton (not Styrofoam or plastic). Cut off the lid and throw it away. Put the bottom of the egg carton on the bottom of the grill. (For a smaller fire just use half.) Put a briquette into each egg cup, and then keep piling briquettes into the carton. Light the egg carton with a match.

A charcoal fire usually starts out with smoke, then flames. When the flames die down, the coals glow red. Then they turn white on the edges. When the edges of about three-quarters of the coals are white, you're ready to cook.

Using a stick or shovel, spread the coals across the bottom of the grill and carefully set the grate on top. Placing a lid over the grill will speed up the cooking time. If the lid has a vent, use it to adjust your fire:

◆ The wider open it is, the faster and hotter the fire burns.

◇ Less open allows a slower burning, cooler fire.

◆ Close it and your fire goes out.

Make Your Own Tin-Can Grill

A tin-can grill is easy and inexpensive to make and can be recycled, thrown away, or reused. Be careful with the can, as the edges are sharp and the metal gets hot. You'll need an adult helper.

What you need:

- a large, clean, empty 1- or 2-pound coffee can
- heavy work gloves
- tin snips
- dirt or sand
- aluminum foil
- metal grate (racks used for cooling cookies work well)

What your adult helper does:

1. Put on gloves!

2. Using the tin snips, cut a line from the open end of the can towards the bottom, stopping 3 inches from the end.

3. Make another cut just like this, 2 inches away from the first cut. Repeat until you get back to the first cut and the circle is completed. Pull the 2-inch strips away from the center. You should have a basket-like holder and access to the center of the can.

What you do:

1. Put on gloves!

2. Pour dirt or sand into the center of the can, about 2 inches deep.

3. Line the center and strips with heavy aluminum foil, creating a big silver bowl. Be careful! The strips are sharp.

4. Place the grate on the strips and carefully push it down so it is level.

5. Remove the grate and place the grill on the ground in a space free of twigs, leaves, or anything else that could burn.

6. Build a charcoal fire right in the grill or use a shovel to carefully transfer hot coals from an existing fire.

7. Replace the grate and cook.

Canyon Sandwiches

MAKE ON THE GRILL

MAIN DISH

SERVES 2

What you need:

- 2 English muffins
- Tomato, sliced
- Avocado, sliced
- Black olives, sliced
- Cheddar cheese, shredded

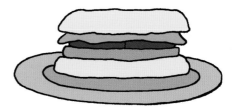

What you do:

1. Split the English muffins and place halves face up on foil.

2. Stack tomato, avocado, and olives on 2 halves.

3. Sprinkle cheese on top.

4. Grill sandwiches open-faced until cheese is melted and bubbly, about 10 minutes.

5. Top with remaining halves and serve.

This recipe can also be made in an oven or on a stovetop.

Asparagus Forest

MAKE ON THE GRILL

SIDE DISH

SERVES 3 TO 4

What you need:

- ◆ 1 bunch asparagus
- ◆ 1/4 cup fresh dill or 1 teaspoon dried dill
- ◆ juice of 1/2 lemon

What you do:

1. Chop an inch off the base of each asparagus spear. Throw away the chopped-off parts.

2. Spread out a layer of aluminum foil that's 4 inches larger than the asparagus.

3. Place the asparagus on the foil. Sprinkle dill on top.

4. Squeeze the lemon juice onto the asparagus.

5. Lay another sheet of foil on top of the asparagus and roll the ends of the foil sheets together so the packet is completely sealed.

6. Place on a grill and cook for about 20 minutes.

This recipe can also be made in a pit or buried in the coals of a fire.

cooking in a can

You can use a can as a pot to cook in over the fire or on a stove or grill. Use a clean, paper-free can of any size. If cooking over a fire, settle the can into the coals. For best results, balance it on three rocks. If the food needs to be covered as it cooks, cover the can with aluminum foil or turn a !arger can upside down over it. After dinner toss the can in the trash or recycle it.

GARBAGE CAN COOKER

You can enclose a fire in a small metal garbage can or a terra cotta pot. Fill the container about halfway full with dirt and then lay some aluminum foil on top. Then build a charcoal fire. You can put a metal rack on top of the coals to make a grill or just cook right on the coals.

BUDDY BURNER

A buddy burner is a small, easy-to-make stove perfect for cooking small amounts of food for one or two hungry campers. You make a buddy burner in a can. You'll want to make yours at least a day in advance.

What you need:

- ◆ short, squat cans (like tuna, pet food, or pineapple cans)
- ◆ corrugated cardboard, free from bright inks, wax, or tape
- ◆ scissors
- ◆ melted wax (see page 23)

What you do:

1. Cut strips of cardboard that are as tall as your can is high. Cut across the corrugation, so you can see the holes in the edge of the cardboard.

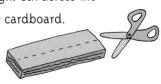

2. Roll up the cardboard and fit it snugly into the can. Cut a thin strip of cardboard $\frac{1}{2}$ inch longer than the can is tall. Put this strip in the spiral so it sticks out of the can. This is your wick.

3. Pour melted wax into the can, almost covering the cardboard. Ta-da! You've made a buddy burner. When you're ready to cook, simply light the wick!

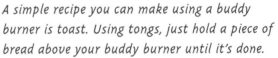

A buddy burner should last for about an hour. When finished, cover your buddy burner with a piece of foil larger than the mouth of the burner to put the fire out. Don't move the burner until the wax is hard and cool.

A simple recipe you can make using a buddy burner is toast. Using tongs, just hold a piece of bread above your buddy burner until it's done.

Howlin' Good Pizza Soup

MAIN DISH
MAKE IN A CAN
SERVES 4 TO 6

What you need:

- ◆ 1 tablespoon butter
- ◆ 1 cup sliced mushrooms, green pepper, onion, or combination
- ◆ 1 cup meat (ground sausage, ground hamburger, or pepperoni chunks)
- ◆ 1 can (15 ounces) tomato sauce
- ◆ 1 can (15 ounces) stewed tomatoes
- ◆ 1 to 2 cups beef broth, vegetable broth, or water
- ◆ shredded mozzarella cheese (optional)
- ◆ goldfish crackers (optional)

What you do:

1. Preheat the can by placing it in or over the heat source. Wear oven mitts and use tongs when handling the hot can.

2. Melt the butter in the can. If your meat is raw, add it to the butter and stir with a wooden spoon or a clean stick until it is well-browned.

3. Add the vegetables and stir until cooked well (about 3 minutes).

4. Add the tomato sauce, tomatoes, and broth. (Add the meat if it's precooked.)

5. Cover your soup with aluminum foil and stir occasionally. Cook until warm, about 15 minutes.

6. Top with mozzarella cheese or goldfish crackers, if using, and serve.

This soup is great served with a grilled cheese sandwich.
You can also make this recipe on a stove or grill.

Apple Stampede

SIDE DISH

MAKE IN A CAN

SERVES 4

What you need:

◆ 4 to 6 medium apples

◆ ½ cup water

◆ ⅓ cup sugar

◆ 2 teaspoons cinnamon

What you do:

1. With your adult helper, peel, core, and cut apples into quarters.

2. Combine apples, water, and sugar in a clean, empty coffee can.

3. Cover with aluminum foil and cook over the fire about 20 minutes or until the apples are soft.

4. With an oven mitt, remove can from heat. Mash sauce with a potato masher, fork, or clean rock.

5. Add cinnamon to taste. Serve warm or cold.

You can also make this recipe on a stove or grill.

cooking in a paper bag or paper cup

You've used paper to start your fire, but have you ever cooked in it? This chapter will teach you how.

COOKING IN A PAPER BAG

If you thoroughly wet a paper bag and wrap your food in it, you can put it on the coals of a fire or on the grill to cook. As long as you rewet it throughout the cooking process it won't catch fire. Try this method for cooking your catch-of-the-day. You'll enjoy some amazingly tender meat.

COOKING IN A PAPER CUP

Pour some water or milk in an unwaxed paper cup and settle it on a buddy burner. This is a quick and easy way to make hot chocolate or tea for one. The liquid keeps the cup from catching fire.

If your cup is too hot to hold, fit it into a second, empty cup.

Rise 'n' Shine Breakfast

MAIN DISH

COOK IN A PAPER BAG ON COALS OR ON THE GRILL

SERVES 1

What you need:

- 2 to 3 strips of bacon
- 1 to 2 eggs
- dry, small lunch-sized brown paper bag
- salt and pepper to taste

What you do:

1. Line the bottom of your bag with the bacon.

2. Crack eggs on top of the bacon. (If you prefer your eggs scrambled, break them into a resealable plastic bag, add some salt and pepper, and squish them around before pouring them on top of the bacon.)

3. Fold the top of the bag down three or four turns, stopping before you reach the food. Spear through the folded part of the bag with a stick and dangle the bag over hot coals. Or you can close the bag and place it bacon-side-down on the grill.

> Why it works: Grease from the bacon coats the bag and keeps it from catching fire!

Porcupine Cocoa
DRINK
MAKE IN A PAPER CUP OVER A BUDDY BURNER
SERVES 4

What you need:

- butter
- 2 ounces unsweetened chocolate squares
- 1/3 cup sugar
- 1/2 cup mini-marshmallows
- 4 Popsicle sticks
- 4 cups milk

What you do at home:

1. Butter four small bowls and lay a Popsicle stick in each.

2. Melt the chocolate following the instructions on the package.

3. Stir in the sugar.

4. Pour equal parts of the chocolate mixture into each of the bowls over the sticks. Add some marshmallows to each.

5. Put the bowls in the freezer.

6. When the chocolate is hard, you should be able to remove the stick, chocolate, and marshmallows (which will all stick together) from the bowls. Now you have 4 chocolate-sicles. Transfer each to a resealable sandwich bag. Keep your chocolate-sicles cool until ready to use.

What you do at your cook site:

1. Warm a cup of milk on the buddy burner.

2. Add a chocolate-sicle.

3. Stir and sip!

This recipe can also be made on the stove.

cooking in leaves and other foods

Leaves and some foods like onions, large mushrooms, tomatoes, green peppers, and oranges make great containers for cooking. They hold in moisture, keeping your meal from burning, as well as adding some zing to your dinner.

Jackrabbit's Bean Burgers

MAIN DISH
COOK IN LEAVES ON THE COALS
SERVES 4

What you need:

- 1 cup canned black beans
- 1/4 cup chopped bell pepper
- 1/4 cup chopped onion
- 1 cup salsa
- 1/2 cup bread crumbs
- 1/3 cup flour
- 2 teaspoons vegetable oil
- 1 tablespoon cilantro
- dash each of salt, pepper, and chili powder
- 8 full leaves of lettuce or cabbage
- 4 hamburger buns and favorite fixin's

What you do:

1. Combine all the ingredients except lettuce leaves, hamburger buns, and fixin's in a gallon-sized freezer bag. Press the air out, seal the bag, and squeeze it to mix.

2. Lay out 4 leaves. Divide the bean mixture into 4 parts. Using your hands, shape them into burgers. Place each burger into a leaf, then cover each with a remaining leaf. Using a long-handled turner, carefully settle the filled leaves onto some medium-hot coals.

3. After about 10 minutes, use a turner to flip the burgers over, and cook for another 10 minutes. Cooking times will vary. Burgers are done when they are hot inside.

4. Put a burger on each bun, add your fixin's, and serve 'em up!

You can also make this recipe on a grill.

Bloomin' Muffins

SIDE DISH

COOK IN ORANGE PEELS ON THE COALS

SERVES 4

What you need:

- 4 medium to large oranges
- 1 egg
- 1/4 cup vegetable oil
- 1 3/4 cups flour
- 1/3 cup sugar
- 2 teaspoons baking powder

What you do:

1. Cut the oranges in half and scoop the insides into a resealable bag. Try not to break or tear the peels. Seal the bag. Set aside the peels.

2. Squeeze the oranges in the bag or roll a smooth rock over them to make orange juice.

3. In another resealable bag, combine the egg and oil with 3/4 cup of the orange juice. Set aside the rest of the juice to drink later.

4. Add the flour, sugar, and baking powder to your bag with the egg and orange juice. Reseal the bag and squeeze the contents thoroughly.

5. Pour the muffin batter into 4 of the orange peel halves, filling about 2/3 full.

6. Using tongs, carefully set the filled orange peels into hot coals. Cook about 30 minutes or until muffins are golden.

You can also make this recipe on a grill.

hot rock cooking

When you cook on a rock, you're really cooking with nature. Rocks soak up heat in your fire and use that energy to make your meal.

Not all rocks make good cooking tools. A good rock:

◆ *is dry. Stay away from rocks in lakes or rivers.*
◆ *is not sedimentary (is not made from a bunch of small rocks and sand).*
◆ *has at least one flat surface.*
◆ *is big enough to cook your food.*
◆ *is small enough for you to carry.*

To cook on a rock, place your rock directly in the hot coals and let it heat for about an hour. It will be extremely hot! Then, using oven mitts *and* tongs, remove the rock from the fire and place it with the flat side up in a dry place free from leaves or grasses that might catch fire. Now you can cook on it.

Once it's cool, wash your rock well before releasing it into the wild.

Sunrise Toast

SIDE DISH
COOK ON A HOT ROCK
SERVES 4

What you need:

◆ vegetable oil
◆ 4 eggs
◆ 8 slices of bread

◆ butter
◆ maple syrup or powdered sugar

What you do:

1. Pour a tablespoon of oil on the hot rock.

2. In a bowl or clean can, beat the eggs together.

3. When the oil is hot, dip a piece of bread in the eggs, coating both sides. Put the coated bread on the rock.

4. When the egg coating on the bottom is cooked, flip the bread over. When both sides are cooked, serve your toast with butter and maple syrup or powdered sugar. Doesn't that rock add flavor?

This recipe can also be made on a stove.

Hot Rock Chicken

MAIN DISH
COOK ON A HOT ROCK
SERVES 6

What you need:

- ◆ 3 rocks (1 big rock that fits inside the chicken and 2 that are slightly larger than your fist)
- ◆ 1 whole chicken
- ◆ barbecue sauce
- ◆ aluminum foil
- ◆ newspaper

What you do:

1. Place the rocks in the fire and leave for 1 hour.

2. Lay out a 2-foot long section of aluminum foil and place the chicken on top.

3. Wearing oven mitts, use tongs to pull the hot rocks out of the fire. Put the big rock inside the chicken and the smaller rocks under each wing.

4. Pour barbecue sauce over the chicken and then wrap the foil around it.

5. Lay out 10 sheets of newspaper and wrap it around the foil. Then cover with another layer of foil. Repeat this 2 more times.

6. Put the chicken in a safe place and let it sit for 3 hours. Unwrap and enjoy! (The chicken is done when it is no longer pink in the center.)

WHY IT WORKS:
The newspaper keeps the heat in while the rocks put heat out. The combination cooks the chicken.

pit cooking

Hot coals buried under dirt create a toasty pit that you can cook food in. When you want to cook in a pit, check the campground rules—some places don't allow you to dig a hole or make a fire ring. To use this method of cooking you have to plan ahead. Some pit cooking recipes take half a day.

To Cook Food in a Pit

◆ Dig a hole 2 to 3 times the size of your cooking containers. Keep the dirt.

◆ Build a fire as described on page 17. Use medium-width logs as your main fuel. Keep adding logs as your fire burns. This takes about an hour. By then your pit should be almost filled with coals.

◆ While the fire is burning, get your food prepared. Food should be placed in a Dutch oven or foil packets.

◆ Ask your adult helper to carefully push the coals to the side of the pit using a shovel.

◆ Put your dinner in the pit (don't let foil packets touch each other) and cover them with about 2 to 3 inches of hot coals.

◆ Lay foil across the top and cover it with a 3-inch layer of dirt.

◆ Once your food is cooked, have your adult helper uncover the pit with the shovel. To get out the packets, scoop well under them with a shovel, being careful not to break the foil.

◆ Using tongs or gloves, shake off packets and open up the foil. Your food will be very hot!

Fawn's Fondue

APPETIZER OR SIDE DISH

COOK IN A PIT

SERVES 4

What you need:

- ◆ 1 loaf of round bread
- ◆ 1 cup shredded cheddar cheese
- ◆ ³/₄ cup cream cheese
- ◆ 1 ½ cups sour cream
- ◆ ½ cup chopped green onions
- ◆ ½ cup canned green chiles
- ◆ raw broccoli, carrots, and cauliflower for dipping

What you do:

1. Lay out a piece of foil that's twice as long as the bread. Place the bread in the center and scoop the soft bread out of the middle, leaving a shell to make a bread "bowl." Leave a ½-inch shell all the way around. Set the scooped-out bread aside.

2. Mix together the cheddar cheese, cream cheese, sour cream, onions, and chiles in a bowl, bag, or can. Pour the mixture into the hollowed-out bread bowl.

3. Bring the edges of the foil together on top of the bread. Wrap the bowl completely with aluminum foil, then cover it with one more layer of foil and place it into the pit.

4. Cook for about 45 minutes. (You'll know it's done when the cheese inside is hot and melted.) Unwrap the foil and eat the dip with the extra bread and veggies. Then eat the bowl!

This recipe can also be made over coals.

Wilderness Wonder Cake

DESSERT

COOK IN A PIT

SERVES 12

What you need:

◆ 1 large package chocolate pudding mix (cooked not instant)

◆ 2¹/₃ cups milk

◆ 1 package chocolate cake mix

◆ 2 cups chocolate chips

What you do:

1. Line a Dutch oven with aluminum foil.

2. In a pot or clean, empty coffee can, combine pudding mix and milk. Stir gently over heat until thick.

3. Remove from heat and stir in cake mix. Pour into Dutch oven. Sprinkle chocolate chips on top and put on lid.

4. Lower the Dutch oven into the pit and cover with foil and dirt. Cook for about 1 hour and 15 minutes.

Try this:

Experiment with pudding and cake flavor combinations. Try vanilla pudding and vanilla cake mix with butterscotch chips on top. Or try chocolate pudding and chocolate cake mix with peanut butter chips.

This recipe can also be made in a solar oven.

solar oven cooking

There's another source of heat you might not have thought of and you can use it for cooking too. What is it? The sun! You can harness the energy of the sun through a solar oven. This chapter will show you how.

Build a Solar Oven

What you need:

- ◆ 2 cardboard boxes (1 should be small enough to fit inside the other with about 2 to 3 inches of space on each side)
- ◆ a piece of cardboard larger than the top of the larger box
- ◆ white Elmer's glue (non-toxic)
- ◆ aluminum foil
- ◆ black construction paper
- ◆ newspaper
- ◆ stapler
- ◆ clear plastic wrap

What you do:

1. Place the large box over the piece of cardboard and trace the size. Then draw a line 2 inches larger in each direction. Cut out the larger shape.

2. Using the glue, cover one side of your cardboard rectangle with aluminum foil. Rub out the wrinkles, making it as smooth as possible. This will be your reflector. Set it aside for now.

3. Place black construction paper in the bottom of the small box.

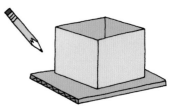

4. Line all the sides of the inside of the small box with foil. Fold the foil over the top edges to keep it in place.

5. Crumple newspaper into a 2- to 3-inch layer in the bottom of the larger box.

6. Set the small box into the larger one. Stuff the spaces in between the two boxes with crumpled newspaper.

7. Staple one side of the reflector to the back of the large box. Your reflector should be able to stand up on its own. If it won't stay up at about a 45-degree angle, try using a pencil, ruler, or dowel to prop it up.

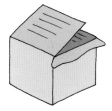

8. Let the oven sit with the reflector facing the sun for about 30 minutes before putting the food inside. When the food is inside, cover the oven opening with plastic wrap to keep the heat in.

The best time to cook with your solar oven is between 10:00 a.m. and 3:00 p.m. Solar ovens are great for fixing lunch. Hot dog!

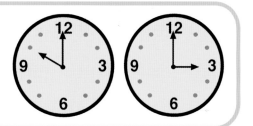

Basking Veggies Pie

MAIN DISH
COOK IN A SOLAR OVEN
SERVES 4 TO 6

What you need:

◆ 2 cups cooked, mixed vegetables (such as carrots, peas, and potatoes)
◆ 1 can cream of mushroom soup
◆ 1 cup biscuit mix
◆ $\frac{1}{2}$ cup milk
◆ 1 egg

What you do:

1. Mix the vegetables with the soup in a clean pie pan.

2. In a bowl or clean, empty can, mix the biscuit mix, milk, and egg together. Pour the mixture on top of the veggies.

3. Place in the oven and cook about 45 minutes, or until the top is golden brown.

This recipe can also be made in a pit if you put the pie pan in a Dutch oven.

Marmot's Munchies

SNACK
COOK IN A SOLAR OVEN
SERVES 12

What you need:

- ◆ 3 cups quick-cooking oats
- ◆ 1 can (14 ounces) sweetened condensed milk
- ◆ 3 cups filling mixture (any combination of chocolate or peanut butter chips, dried cranberries or raisins, peanuts or almonds, and/or coconut)
- ◆ 3 tablespoons butter
- ◆ Muffin tin

What you do:

1. Mix oats, sweetened condensed milk, and filling mixture together in a large bowl.

2. Using 1 tablespoon of butter, grease the insides of the muffin tin.

3. Melt the remaining butter in a pie pan or small can and stir into oat mixture.

4. Press the mixture into each of the muffin cups.

5. Put the muffin pan in your solar oven and bake for 30 minutes. Let cool before serving.

This recipe can also be made in a pit if you put the muffin pan in a Dutch oven.

Spit Cooking

A spit helps food cook evenly. You can make your own spit out of skewers, a clean metal coat hanger, a green stick with the bark removed, or even a wooden dowel. The kind of spit you use depends on what materials you have and how heavy the food you are cooking is. Simply spear foods (such as vegetables, fruit, or even a whole chicken) and then turn your spit over the fire.

You can work a spit in three ways:

1. Drive two forked sticks into the ground on either side of a fire and lay the ends of the spit in the "y"s.

2. Balance the ends of the stick on the rims of a Garbage Can Cooker (see page 32).

3. Lay spit across a grill.

Roly-Poly Mushrooms

SIDE DISH
MAKE ON A SPIT
SERVES 4

What you need:

◆ ¹/₂ pound ground beef
◆ 2 tablespoons butter
◆ ¹/₂ cup bread crumbs
◆ 1 cup shredded cheddar cheese
◆ 8 large fresh mushrooms
◆ wooden or metal skewers

What you do:

1. In a Dutch oven or on a stove, cook the beef until it's brown.

2. Add the butter, bread crumbs, and cheese. Mix well.

3. Wash the mushrooms and remove the stems.

4. Thread one mushroom onto a skewer, with the open part facing you.

5. Spoon some of the meat mixture into the mushroom.

6. Thread a second mushroom onto the skewer, with the open part facing the first one. This should enclose the meat mixture.

7. Repeat with the remaining mushrooms, using more skewers if needed.

8. Balance skewers across the fire. Turn occasionally and cook until warm.

This recipe can also be made right on the grill.

Tropical Kebobs

MAIN DISH
MAKE ON A SPIT
SERVES 1

What you need:

◆ Pineapple chunks
◆ Mandarin orange slices
◆ Cooked ham chunks or lunch
   meat
◆ Teriyaki sauce

What you do:

1. Spear a pineapple chunk, orange slice, and piece of ham on a skewer.
   Repeat until your skewer is filled. Drizzle with teriyaki sauce.

2. Balance skewers across the fire. Turn occasionally and cook until warm.

Try this:

You can make a sweet dessert tropical kebob by replacing the ham and
teriyaki with pieces of pound cake drizzled with honey and rolled in coconut
flakes. Cook on a spit until warmed through.

This recipe can be made on the grill.

Dutch oven cooking

Dutch ovens are heavy cast-iron pots with lids. They come in all different sizes and are often used in camp cooking.

There are two basic kinds of Dutch ovens—one has a rounded lid and a flat bottom, and the other has legs and a flat lid. The first type is most often used over a stove. The second type (which is also called a camp oven) is used in a campfire nestled in the coals. Either type can be used in a cooking pit.

 If you buy a new Dutch oven, follow the manufacturer's instructions to season it. Seasoning it keeps your food from sticking and scorching. To cook in a Dutch oven, simply toss the food inside and put the lid on. If you're using the kind that goes on the stovetop, simply put it on the stove to cook. If you're cooking over the coals, carefully lower your Dutch oven into the ashes of a fire. Then, using a shovel, scoop some hot coals onto the lid.

Winter Stew

MAIN DISH
MAKE IN A DUTCH OVEN
SERVES 6 TO 8

What you need:

◆ 2 tablespoons flour

◆ 1 pound beef, cut into $^{3}/_{4}$-inch cubes

◆ 2 tablespoons butter

◆ 3 cups vegetable broth

◆ 6 cups sliced vegetables (onions, carrots, potatoes, green beans, and/or corn)

What you do:

1. Place the lid on the empty Dutch oven and set it in the coals. When the oven is hot, remove it with an oven mitt and remove the lid.

2. Add the meat, flour, and butter and stir to brown the meat, about 5 minutes.

3. Add the broth, put the lid on, and settle the Dutch oven back into the coals, shoveling some extra coals on top. Cook for about an hour.

4. Using newspaper, carefully sweep the coals off the lid. Wearing oven mitts, remove the lid.

5. Add the vegetables. Put the lid back on and pile some coals back on top.

6. Leave the Dutch oven in the coals for another 45 minutes.

You can also make this recipe in a can.

Geyser Cake

DESSERT
MAKE IN A DUTCH OVEN
SERVES 6 TO 8

What you need:

◆ 1 can apple pie filling

◆ 1 package spice cake mix

◆ 1 can lemon-lime soda or ginger ale

What you do:

1. Line a Dutch oven with aluminum foil.

2. Put the fruit along the bottom.

3. Mix the cake mix and soda together in a bowl or clean, empty coffee can. Pour the batter on top of the fruit.

4. Put the lid on the Dutch oven and set it in the coals. Cover with hot coals and cook for about 45 minutes.

Try this:

Combine different fruits and flavors. For example, try chocolate cake mix with cherry pie filling, or white cake mix with canned pineapple or peaches.

You can also make this recipe in a solar oven.

Collect 'em All!

Available at bookstores or directly from

GIBBS SMITH, PUBLISHER

1.800.748.5439 / www.gibbs-smith.com